WHERE FIREFLIES DARE

A JOURNEY OF COURAGE, RESILIENCE, QUEST FOR SELF-REALISATION, AND ITS LINK WITH THE INFINITE COSMOS.

SAMIT DHAR

Made with ♥ on the Notion Press Platform
www.notionpress.com

Contents

Preface

Every story begins with a quiet moment, a breath before the storm. The pages that follow are born from such moments—whispers of a past long buried, stirring to life once more. This tale is not merely about the events that unfold, but about the spaces between them—the silences that hold the most profound truths.

Set in a place where time seems to stand still, this story explores the unseen forces that shape our lives, often unnoticed, but always present. The characters you will meet are not heroes in the traditional sense. They are ordinary individuals—haunted by their choices, driven by forces beyond their control, and tethered to a history they cannot escape.

At its heart, this narrative delves into the fragile line between reality and what lies beyond. It speaks of secrets buried in the dark, of memories that refuse to fade, and of the inevitable pull of fate. As the events unravel, you may find that the answers you seek are not always the ones you want, and the darkness, once revealed, may be more familiar than you'd care to admit.

This book invites you to step into a world where the past lingers like a shadow, waiting to be unearthed. It asks only one thing of you: to look beyond the surface, to listen to the quiet hum of the unknown, and to embrace the journey into the unseen.

The story is yours now.

Prologue

Where Fireflies Dare' follows a teacher from a AWES school who unexpectedly finds himself in the world of paratroopers, set against the stark deserts of Rajasthan and the dense jungles of the hilly terrain in the far northeast.

Selected for a special operation for his unique linguistic skills and adventurous spirit, he undergoes rigorous training with the Lightfoot unit, where he faces challenges that push his physical, mental limits.

As he adopts to military life, he wrestles with his identity, family expectations, his changing surroundings, circumstances. He faces a struggle trying to unify the different worlds, of a soldier, of a teacher, of a wanderer in search of spiritual salvation.

CHAPTER ONE

WHERE FIREFLIES DARE

The bitter, cold wind with the airborne shingle cut into my face as I descended into the dark below. The dropper was no longer visible, only its faint humming sound could be heard. My eyes were saved because of the protective glasses. This part of Rajasthan was famous for frequent sandstorms. On descending, I rolled a bit and sank into knee-deep sand. I managed my parachute and went along to the marked point. The rest of the Lightfoot unit of seven must have landed nearby. Soon, I found them led by Sergeant Bahari. The sergeant jeered at me, a teacher from the AWES, daring to jump with professional soldiers. It was an unpleasant surprise for them from the top brass. This was my 13th jump with them as I gained experience as a paratrooper.

Strikes strange? A teacher, a paratrooper? Well, I was surprised at myself when I was picked up in a screening test by the army intelligence, which was held under the guise of regular promotions in the AWES. After about half a month from the test date, one fine morning, as I was taking a revision class of class XII, a messenger from the principal's office handed me a letter which contained an address of Chandigarh cantonment, and I was ordered to report within 72 hours. When I met the Principal, he told me that he had already been served a letter to release me, and it was from very high up. I did not know why such urgency had come up. The AWES had never given me such orders before. In Chandigarh, three very sharp-looking men were sitting on the other side of the table going through my records. One of the starred guys spoke to me in Putonghua. I replied, and he was pleased to hear my fluency. The others spoke in Yue, Xiang, Min, Gan, Wu, Kejia. I was thorough in these languages, after Bengali, English, and Hindi. Another big-faced guy in stars asked me about my oriental looks, puffy eyes. I said my parents were both Bengalis; I had no far-fetched connections to Mongoloids even in my ancestors. They asked why I had done so much in the Chinese language as my records showed. I had an M.A and M.Phil in English from the North Bengal University, yet strangely, I was so much interested in Chinese and Tibetan. I said that though I loved English Literature, I had a strong, inquisitive mind for the teachings of Buddha from my college days. It was this interest that led me to Ladakh and Bhutan when I was unemployed and stayed there for a couple of years in villages outside monasteries, teaching village children, earning my bread somehow, and was allowed in thrice a week to learn from benevolent monks. Moreover, I took Chinese language courses and obtained certificates from Gurgaon, New Delhi, and later on Chennai. I completed from HSK1 to advanced proficiency level of HSK6. I was also thorough with Dzongkha, the Sino-Tibetan language spoken by Bhutanese people.

After the interview, the starred guys offered me a promotion which I was nervous about but could not deny.

They told me that I would be on probation for a year, and if I succeeded, I would be given special jobs, and if I failed, I would be returned to the AWES. Leave for the next 365 days was strictly forbidden. My parents were very displeased and told me to reject the offer somehow, but I felt that it would be a chance to have a glimpse into another world. It would be risky but thrilling. After all, I always wanted a life different from the beaten track. During my Bedouin-type lifestyle in various parts of Bhutan and Ladakh, I had caused a lot of tears and anguish for my parents as they appealed to me to return to regular life, get a job, get married, and settle down. I lent a deaf ear and concentrated on the Buddhist scriptures. After a couple of years, I moved in with the AWES after clearing stringent examinations.

I was moved in with the Lightfoot unit, a small unit of ten men at a military station somewhere in the hills near Mount Abu. The guys were tough enough to kill a bull, and I was no match for them. The only thing they could not defeat me in was Chess. I had a knack for it since my childhood and was pretty good at it during my years of service in the AWES. I remember one of the riflemen in the Lightfoot unit; he was an excellent sharpshooter. He was the only one who thought that I was an asset to the unit, and the rest of them took me as a burden.

Soon six months were over, and I earned my wings, the parachute logo. I was a paratrooper and belonged to the Lightfoot unit. An entry into an entirely different world. I never thought this would become of me someday. It was like a reincarnation into another life. The bookworm sitting in a silent library and a humming class was reincarnated into a firefly to move about in a world that was fully unknown to him. We were sent off to the northeast in

Arunachal for special mountain warfare training. In a soft station during routine training, I was injured while sliding down a rope from a chopper and was sent to the infirmary. The chief nurse there, Dippanita Ghosh, was known as Nightingale for her dedication and nursing skills, her only peculiarity being her excessive anger with any of her assistants who neglected duty or wounded army personnel who did not listen to her advice while being treated. That day when I sat with bleeding hands, she came in gracefully, cut off my gloves, took away the skin that had peeled off, dressed and bandaged the wound. It was painful, but her beauty and graceful skill were comforting. I had the guts to say that if she did not mind, I would thank her by offering her a cup of coffee and cakes at the station mess. She looked at me indignantly and bluntly refused. I thought I had been too brave. I should have thanked her in some other way.

After a week of classes on speaking Tibetan, Chinese, and Dzongkha language to my friends, we returned to the usual field and jungle training. I was learning fast how not to get caught up in a wild spin while getting down from a chopper via rope. The rifleman and I played chess at our mess for an hour after dinner. One day, one of the top brass who was in the selection board at Chandigarh paid a visit and called us up to brief about a hit-and-run mission at an undisclosed location at a terrorist camp in Myanmar, just two kilometers from the international border. It would be completed under the cover of darkness; we were to use silent weaponry. Targets would be sitting outside around a fire, and we were to identify them via infrared binoculars, camera, hit, and rush to the extraction point to meet the small bell chopper. On the designated day, we were taken aboard. After 15 minutes of nap of the earth flying, we dropped down. We jogged for 33 minutes and reached the spot. A scout and reconnaissance guy guided us to the target point. I was almost out of breath; I had trained well, but the terrain was too uneven.

On reaching the spot, three were positioned as snipers. One was to sit like a bird on a tree and watch over the entire party and scan the area so that we did not get caught from behind by a night patrol. The laser range finder and infrared camera were to be handled by me. I was sitting behind a log and looking down on the terrorist camp, with the enemy relaxing around a fire. They had no idea that we were there. I confirmed three targets. I had to crawl and point out the targets to the three snipers, radio silent. The bodies of the three targets lay in a pool of blood as the others ran for cover. We withdrew silently and began jogging back. The chopper was waiting for us. Just as I was about to board it, my left foot fell into a small hole, and my ankle was in severe pain. I was helped up; the rifleman who played chess with me also had slashed his flesh on the right arm; he had fallen somewhere while returning. The top brass congratulated us on a debriefing at the base. After a medical check-up, the rifleman and I were referred to the hospital. I was happy in pain, knowing I would get to meet Dipannita Ghosh. I called back home in Siliguri, and my parents were happy to hear my voice. I did not tell them anything about the injury. As I lay on the hospital bed with a lot of pain in my ankle, Dipannita came in with her daily checklist. I complained about why the pain was not reducing and why I was not being given painkillers. She replied in a stern voice that painkillers were not good at all. The sprain would take time to heal, and I was to remain satisfied with a crepe bandage and hot and cold baths for my foot every eight hours. She went away swiftly before I could say anything more.

The rifleman was just across the corridor, recovering faster than me. I wanted to play chess with him. One evening I had a visitor from my unit; he brought some chocolates for us and a small chess board. That evening, when I limped my way to the rifleman's cabin, I didn't know that the head nurse would return for a last round before retiring to her quarters for the night. We were just twenty minutes into the game when she appeared and straight away ordered me to go back to my cabin. I thought she would lend me her shoulder to help me get back, but she looked on indifferently as I limped back to my cabin. She said that if I repeated this the next time, I would be given a discharge certificate and returned to my quarters for active duty with a painful, limping foot. That night I lay half awake in pain and remembered my school-time sweetheart. She was a smart lady now working somewhere in southern India as a junior manager in a pharmaceutical company. She was married to a tall, handsome guy, pretty famous as a company consultant. Well, I never proposed to her; I just fantasized about her, watched her from class nursery to X before we moved off to different schools to study in higher grades. She always stood first or sometimes second in the class and was very polite and friendly. Many of us boys had a crush on her, but no one ever dared to tell her. My school days in Siliguri were wonderful. I remember a guy named Shyam; he too had a crush on her and used to sit next to me in class and tell me how he thought he would marry her once he became an adult. We were in class VIII when one day Shyam told me how he fantasized about her at night and couldn't sleep. I was jealous and angry about this.

Those days, we were pretty mad about playing Superman and Batman. We used red and black capes to dress up as Superman and Batman. One day, I had a naughty idea of teaching a lesson to Shyam for saying so many things about the girl who was my heartthrob. That day we were playing Batman and Superman as usual on the school ground, where some sort of construction work was going on. There were pieces of wood and bamboo and slender ropes. I told Shyam that the black cape he had bought would look better if it was fixed on his shoulder with some pieces of wood or bamboo. He agreed. I tied both his hands along with the cape on a four-foot-long bamboo. He was puzzled as to why I had tied his hands tightly with the bamboo. I said that it would appear that he was a real Batman. He complained that he wouldn't be able to use his hands freely. I convinced him. We played. The break was over, and all the students went back to class; only I and Shyam were left behind. When Shyam told me to untie his hands, I just pulled down his pants and ran to the class. He went on yelling, but I didn't listen. After a period, the Headmistress, Mrs. Petrie, came in. She brought along with her Shyam, who had a red face, and his eyes were red and watery. Of course, his pants were not down anymore. Shyam pointed at me. I had a thorough dose that afternoon at the Principal's office. When the class came to know the whole episode the next day, all had a good laugh, but the stripes that were made by the cane of Mrs. Petrie burned on my bums for a week.

Dipannita was so unlike my school sweetheart. She was haughty, always in a fiery mood. Well, when her subordinates came in to attend to the patients, they always spoke highly of the Head Matron, for her skills, discipline, and honest, straightforward nature. One of the nurses wanted to learn the Chinese alphabets from me, and I took a class of fifteen minutes every day when she came in according to the hospital duty rosters. While teaching her, I learned quite a few things about Dipa, who was the only daughter of her father. She hailed from Metelli in Doars. Her father was not an army man but worked in a government enterprise named the Jute Corporation of India. One afternoon, as I was teaching the nurse to write the Chinese alphabets, Dipannita came in. I thought I would soon be reported. She just told the subordinate to go out. She looked deep into my eyes and said it was unbelievable that I was so indisciplined in spite of being in the army. Well, I told her about myself being a teacher in the AWES. She did not believe that a teacher could be fit enough to go in for special operations and survive. She said something about someone with whom she was once engaged. He was in the Para Special Forces. I was eager to know why she said "once engaged." She bluntly told me that it was none of my concern.

I was released and started my normal life in my unit. The day began with the usual exercises, and after breakfast, we had our special mountain warfare training sessions. After lunch, we were taken to the station hall, where we were given theoretical knowledge about the long mountainous terrain of the border with China, its vegetation, wildlife, and the way of life of the village people living in the dense jungles where the Indian, Bhutanese, and Chinese armies often came face to face with each other. We learned about a new area in the North Eastern Lhuntse in Bhutan, where the Bhutanese and Chinese borders converged, though it was no man's land, -'The Bee Loud Ground'. This was a place where many of the un-uniformed Indian army personnel who went in for covert reconnaissance missions never returned. The nearest villagers who lived fifteen kilometers from this area referred to it as a place where they often heard the low humming of bees and never dared walk into the area. They said that it was a place where poisonous bees lived. The intelligence thought that there must have been some sort of machinery set up by the Chinese. Radar, satellite surveillance, however, never showed any kind of unidentified vehicles or personnel in and around that area. It was a mystery.

One evening, after a bout of chess with my unit guys, I went off for a long ride to the nearby town of Bomdilla on my Enfield. I went to the local library and read. I went to a coffee shop that made much better coffee than our mess at the station. While returning from the town, when I was just about five kilometers away from the station, I saw Dipa standing at a bus stop waiting for the Army bus that was scheduled to arrive there within some minutes. I stopped and courageously said if I could give her a lift to the station. I expected that she would bluntly turn me down, but she did not. I was more than surprised. As she sat on the pillion seat, she kept a safe distance so that her body would not touch mine even when I went over speed breakers. I asked her what she had bought. She said it was none of my concern. I said I was sorry to have asked. She replied I should not be. Well, she was more than a minefield, unpredictable. Well, that ride was a wonderful one for me. I dropped her off at her quarters.

Within the next twenty days, my unit and I were busy learning to live in the jungles without any resupplies from the Army Supply Corps. We were given twelve, 100 gm glucose packets, some small packets of biscuits, chocolates, first aid, water purifier chemicals, and left for days in the jungle about 69 kms from the station. It was very tough. We were given instructions on how to select the right plants in the jungle, especially the ones which grew in the high regions of the northeastern borders with China, which could nourish us in times of zero resupplies. The Major who took charge during the training had a long experience with the Naga regiment. He was thorough with Dzongkha and Chinese languages. Along with many other things, he taught us how to use doses of antivenom if bitten by snakes. The biggest trouble was leeches while we went up the trees to put up a sniper nest or to get a good look at the surrounding area. I remember one occasion when I had sixteen leeches pulled out from my knees and neck by the other guys in my unit. The Lightfoot unit was really learning to be lightfoot, that is, to remain without any trace, undetected for days in the dense jungles, spotting dummy targets, and neutralizing them. We learned to use the latest sat phones, the latest infrared, night vision equipment, explosives with motion sensors, and of course, the American 5.56x45mm caliber FN SCAR L assault rifle. My chess buddy, the rifleman, gave me a lesson on some of his favorites, the XM250 automatic by Sig Sauer, the .223 Remington rifle, and the Ruger Precision rifle (6.5 Creedmoor) with a Vortex Viper HS-T Scope. We learned how to make rabbit snares, the jungle was filled with them, and we had no scarcity of protein. During rains, we put on our camouflaging rain gear. The most difficult part was the fear of getting bitten by centipedes or snakes while we slept. Of course, we had a special kind of odorless ointment that we put on to protect ourselves, yet we could not overcome the fear of insects crawling into our ears or nose during sleep. When the training session ended, we all had lost three to four kilos of weight. Four of us had stomach problems.

On our arrival back at the station, I was eager to be referred for a medical check-up at the hospital rather than lining up at a doctor's camp near our mess. I had applied for a leave of 15 days. It had been more than a year since I had been home. There was no response yet from the higher-ups. I was not referred to the hospital, but I decided to visit myself. When I reached the reception area, I saw Dipannita in plain clothes coming out of the Chief Medical officer's office. She looked at me strangely. I put on a smile. She did not. She stopped and told me that the training had been good for me as it had reduced my extra kilos, and I was medically more fit than before. I said that if she had no shift that day, maybe I could take her to the nearby town of Bomdila, and we could have a cup of coffee. She said that she was not interested in riding my bike, but if I was interested in packing, then I could lend her a helping hand at her quarters. She was to pack some gifts for her family as she was going to her hometown in Metelli, on leave for 19 days. I was more than happy. Her place was neatly decorated. There was a harmonium. I told her that I was surprised and impressed to see that she had time and talent to practice that. She said that she hardly had time but tried to find some to play it. She talked about the days when her parents had engaged a music teacher for her music lessons. How she performed in programs in her locality while at school, and how she had passed the various examinations of the Bangiya Sahitya Parishad. I looked at the music discs and Bengali novels in her living room. She made lemon tea and omelette, it was refreshing. On my appreciation of the tea, she said men are all alike; they try too much to impress the girl they want, and when they have had their fill, they simply discard them. I said I was not one of them. She said that time would prove it. She said that with my excessive talkative nature and a too smiley face, I was not fitting well into the shoes of an army man. When I talked about my past career, she said I was just a wanderer. I said that I was just a firefly, small yet fiery. She laughed and said I thought too highly about myself; I was just another Bengali Babu of a 'Mache Bhatey' nature.

As we talked on, I found that she belonged to a simple middle-class family. She seemed to be very fond of her father as she said how he was the one who pleated her saree, plaited her long hair when she was in the senior classes, and how he bought jalebis and samosas almost every day in the evening for her. On freezing winter evenings, she would open the door for her father only after he showed her the packet of sweets through the window. Her mother was a housewife who fed her by hand every day when she returned from school. It was 8 PM when we bid each other goodnight, and I returned to my quarters.

On my bed, I lay awake for long hours that night, thinking about her and my floating life. Well, in the whole world, I only had Pop and Mom to feel my absence. Of course, there was another person—that was the rifleman. He had become a close friend of mine. He honed his skills in the target field every day. He had a feeling that soon we would be sent to a covert mission at the Chinese border adjoining Bhutan. I was thinking something else, that is, of taking a leave, visiting my home at Siliguri, and perhaps Dipa's home when she would be there.

We were being fed Samudashi and Emadashi for days, along with edible herbs that grow in the high mountains of Bhutan, and were bored. One day, the rifleman had finished four sets of firing tests, and I was his marker. While having lunch at the target field, he showed me photos of his family—his parents, his wife, two kids. His home in a village 36 kilometers from Ziro with deep gorges and far-flung valleys. His longing to get back home at least for a week that year was evident in his talk. Coincidentally, the commander the next day told us that we could avail of a 9-day leave to visit our homes.

It had been a long time since I saw my parents. I rang home, and my parents were eager to see me. Before departing, I went to the infirmary and met Dipannita's colleague, the nurse whom I had taught Chinese for a few days. I took Dipannita's number.

On reaching Siliguri, I merrily walked down the alleys to my home. Mom had cooked dishes more than I could eat. Strict diet and learning to survive on too little had shrunk my appetite to the bare minimum. The way my parents were living seemed to me very unfamiliar. Though just a year ago, it seemed very cozy and comfortable for me when I came on my vacations. I loved to sleep, sit along with my parents before the television and watch the news and serials for hours. I loved to visit my relatives' and friends' houses, even though most of my friends were away in other cities following their jobs. When I would meet them by chance, they were polite, but they seemed to lack that years-old touch of deep feelings; they seemed to have moved away into their new sphere of highly paid jobs in mega cities and a bunch of fresh friends. Was I too, slowly, unconsciously withdrawing from my known world and speeding into a new one? How could I be less in emotions, sentiments, longing for staying in my hometown with my parents? It should not be. It did not feel right. Earlier, when I served in Margaret High School in Siliguri as a guest teacher, Maharaj in charge of the school and hostel under RKVA had offered me to join the same, accept the saffron dress, be austere, be a saint. He told me that with my free and energetic mind, I would be an asset to the ashram and would be able to serve the general people in a more selfless and effective way. I did not choose it. I loved my world of materialism, family, friends, fancy watches, fashionable dresses, sports shoes, perfumes, chicken tandoori, and my bike rides with my admirers. I loved to be a part of a world of adventure, a thrilling career. I thought of joining the army. I got into it but on the less thrilling part, AWES. Detachment with my parents and my hometown was never even imagined by me. I always longed for them. Now there seemed to be a change in me. Is it possible for one to change worlds so easily? Was I more at home with my unit, the army mess, the rifleman before me with a chessboard, the clandestine operations, the infirmary, and Dippanita Ghosh? My face for my hometown, friends, parents, and relatives was shriveling up but becoming bouncy, smooth, and radiant on the other plane. It becomes too difficult to remain the same in different planes simultaneously for such a materialistic man like me. The Maharaj at RKVA had said about shedding the materialistic cloth and becoming a finer creature with a finer spirit much above the base, but I chose to be an ordinary man and live among the base.

The bus to Metelli was overcrowded, and time moved like a turtle as the bus stopped every now and then to drop and pick up passengers. The small town consisted of a small market, some small alleys with wooden and a few concrete houses with tin roofs. Almost all the houses had a front yard with flowering plants and a small kitchen garden at the back. I had not made a phone call to Dipannita, as I knew she would never approve of me coming to her hometown and meeting her. While in the market, I went to a grocery store, mentioned her name, her job, and a few words about her father. It was a small place where everyone knew everyone. Soon, I was walking down one of the narrow alleys. I stood in front of a small house with wild roses growing in abundance along with other seasonal flowers. An old man, tall-figured, slender, very fair in complexion, with glasses, in a Lungi and shirt, was bending down and watering the plants. I asked about Dipannita. He said he was her father, smiled, and came forward. I told him about myself. He said that his daughter had mentioned about me once or twice, being the only other Bengali serving there in that small military station. He ushered me in. I met his wife, who seemed busy with her household chores. She told me to sit as her daughter had gone to the market and would soon be back. Dipannita's father was pleased to see and talk to me. He asked all about my hometown, my parents, and how I ventured into active military service. While listening about my student life and my career, he expressed astonishment as to whether I never thought systematically about my life, and was it not enough for me to settle down? When his wife came after finishing her cooking, she was inquisitive too. She requested me to have lunch, and I could not say no. I heard the gate open, and Dipannita came in with a bag full of vegetables and groceries. She looked at me, but she did not have any surprise in her eyes as I had expected. She casually asked me how I found out her house and how everything was there back at the military station. Her father was away for a few minutes and soon returned with a plate of rosogollas. He insisted that being a young man, I should finish off all of them. We four sat for an hour discussing how things were in the northeast and whether the skirmishes with China would end in the near future. At the dining table, Dipannita's mother served me the veggies and fish. Dipa too ladled rice and an extra fish onto my plate. After the lunch, when I wanted to leave, Dipa's father told me to take the 4.30 PM bus from Metelli market as it halted much less compared to the other ones. It was only 2 PM, so we sat again and chatted. I expressed my wonder at the garden they had and also the adjoining houses. I said that I always dreamt of having such a house for myself, but it never became a reality. Dipa commented that I, being a city boy, would not be able to live more than a month in such a quiet place like Metelli. I countered and said that with a year of active service in the Lightfoot unit, I had grown habituated to life in small, quiet places. The old man again brought a plate of rosogollas before me. I said it would not be possible. Dipannita's mother said that her husband was obsessed with rosogollas, and he being a gastro patient, did not have outside food and lived only on home-cooked veggies and fish curry with less of everything, but had rosogollas every day. The old man said that on my next visit to Metelli, I should bring rosogollas from a particular shop in Siliguri. I laughed and said I would bring a pot full of them. Dipannita's parents were very free and frank, friendly. I wondered at their fine spirit of making me feel so much at home, though it was my first visit.

While returning, the old lady packed some green, fresh lemons, sweet papaya that had grown in their garden. She said that their daughter would soon be away on duty. Probably I would also be in the same. She told me to come down to their place whenever I came on leave to Siliguri. She added that in their world of old age, they both looked for some sweet moments with their daughter, and if possible, with me, as I was almost like their son. While walking down to the market from where I would board the bus, Dipa accompanied me. She said that it was a small place, and their neighbors would soon be talking about me. After I got the address from the grocery shop, she had gone to the same, where the shopkeeper had told her about me enquiring about her. She said that her parents were too simple and honest, but I should not frequent this place without her permission as she did not want any unnecessary talk going about me and her in the unpolluted air of Metelli. Well, I did not take her seriously. It was a short time, but I had come to know about her reservedness. As I got into the bus, I said that if she could come down to Siliguri at my home, my old parents would also be happy. She replied that she would not have such plans and would meet me only at the station after 9 days when she would return. I said, in that case, I would come here again next weekend. She looked at me sternly. I laughed and added that it was just a joke. As the bus started, she stood below the window and said I should not mind any negative things she said, "I am of a different nature, you will be able to understand me with the passage of time." I smiled back and nodded. As I moved, the tea gardens of Metelli looked like a new universe with slow, calm, green planets surrounding a bright Sun.

Krishna was playing his flute, which he had done innumerable times in his limitless kingdom of multiverses. I, along with the others of the unit, were called back before the full leave was over. At the soft station, we received a message of a briefing. Our mobile phones were to be switched off, and no communication was to be done with anyone outside the small periphery of our team. The daily classes of Bhutanese and Chinese languages were expected to have borne fruit. We were given a short and sharp oral, written, and listening test. All performances were not satisfactory to the top brass. The guns, ammunition, and explosives we were trained on would not be of any use. The top brass seemed particularly interested in the so-called Bee Loud Ground. This area was about seventy-five square kilometers of inaccessible, foul weather terrain. This area was a favorite among Indian reconnaissance and scout teams to peek into the Chinese side. Nine expert personnel had gone missing without a trace in this area. A final team of three was selected: my buddy, the rifleman, me, and our trainer, the major from the Naga regiment. We would travel on foot to a spot 39 km from the "Bee Loud Ground." Further instructions would reach us from the top brass in coded form via local agents.

It was the month of May, and the dress of a Bhutanese herder was comfortable, except for the buzzing mosquitoes and wasps that attacked my feet as we moved along the valley bushes. In Gelephu, we were introduced to a soldier of the Royal Bhutanese army who would escort us north of Punakha and later introduce us to a group of high-altitude mountain herders, the Zhops, as monks from the monastery at Gelephu, traveling to the different secluded parts of the northeastern Lhuntse, inaccessible parts of Bhutan close to the Chinese border just for worship and meditation. At the monastery at Gelephu, there were contacts who ensured that any sort of inquiry about our identities would give out convincing results.

As we moved upwards following the summer movement of foraging, the Zhops were very inquisitive. They had questions on God, Buddha, and the afterlife. It was really enjoyable for me to answer them. However, few of them could understand when I explained certain excerpts from Buddhism. We would travel on foot to a spot from where the "Bee Loud Ground" would be 39 kilometers away. Further instructions would reach us from the top brass in coded form via local agents. We three were together till the border of Bumthang and Lhuntse district. A local agent brought new orders. The coded message was written in the form of numbers and signs on pieces of prayer flags. I was to continue alone up the heights towards the extreme northeast section of Lhuntse and carry out my reconnaissance work. The rifleman and the major made a U-turn. The terrain of Lhuntse is so uneven and remote that it becomes difficult even for the Bhutan government to carry out social welfare projects. There are roughly 15,000 Bhutanese in the scattered far-flung villages across the steep mountains and deep valleys.

The meal of boiled carrots, rock salt with some Ema Datshi, and smelly butter was available at night when we camped, and during the day, we had wild sour berries, carrots, and dried yak milk. There was another delicacy that was eaten when we met other herders on our way—Samu datshi. I kept away from it. I thought that wild mushrooms in this dish would cause an allergy, as I had already avoided it at the station at Bomdilla. At night, it would get pretty cold even inside the skin tents. I had a yak wool blanket, a big polythene sheet for rain protection, and some copies of Buddhist scriptures on meditation. The major from the Naga regiment insisted on being lean while we sneaked into the forbidden areas of the Bhutan-China border. After three days into the journey, a day came when I had a burning forehead. I was tense. The herders realized my tension and laughed. They said I was a monk but behaving like a child. We reached a village at about 9,300 feet just within the tree line. A village doctor put his ear on my chest, listened, went away, and brought back beetle shaped dried herbal paste, which I was to have as a single dose thrice a day. That night, the villagers wanted to hear about the great Buddha from me. I could not talk much, but they were pretty impressed and fed me Bathup—a hot spinach soup and cereal grain beer. I burned in the cold night. I remembered the conversation between Swami Vivekananda and Sister Nivedita, who had ventured into a new religion of Hinduism from Christianity. They discussed how each man may learn about God in his own language, in his own way. Swamiji was also of the opinion that his disciples were not to be forced to follow his thought stream. Kali could be seen from other angles too. But all necessarily boiled down to the point that life was just a book, at the end of which we realize that it meant nothing. I thought in the light of that, where was I? What quintessence of life had I understood? As the night wind whistled outside, I remained half awake, and images of my parents, the top brass, the rifleman, Dipannita, Maharaj at Margaret, and the Principal of my junior school, Mr. Nelson Petrei, whirled around. Each glimpse had their own catchy dialogues from their own angle of views about me and what I should do and what I should not. I thought I was near expiry. Maybe I would depart, and my physical mask would be buried in these slopes. Life and death danced around. I was like a firefly in the vast dark, flying to find my universe among the many, to be reborn again.

The village doctor told me that I needed rest. My commanders had told me to finish the mission within 18 days and be back. I was on my feet after 19 hours. There was weakness and light wheezing, and my target was first the Bee Loud Ground and then the secret Chinese listening station at 11,000 ft.

As we climbed further up, we had a sudden halt as two yaks were missing. Dusk was fast approaching, and the herders were tense about the fate of the two yaks. They feared that Big Foot might have taken them away. This was a term I had read in books earlier but never gave much thought. I asked whether they had ever seen it. They denied it but claimed that even their forefathers had mentioned Big Foot. They had heard its shrill cries sometimes in the areas just below the snow line and found stone, twigs structures, surprisingly in an organized form along their ancient routes. Even small children who wandered off into the forest from villages often vanished without a trace. There was a fear of the unknown in their eyes. It disturbed their peaceful, slow, calm world. The next day, I left the herders and went on my way with the coded map on the prayer flags and navigated with the position of the Sun. At dusk, I was 13 kilometers away from the Bee Loud Ground and decided to set my camp, with the polythene sheet and twigs from nearby trees. I had some dried berries, yak milk solids, and corn that would see me through for 9 days. At night, I was too tense to sleep. However, nothing crept up to my camp except my fear of Big Foot. I fell asleep at dawn and woke up when it was about 7 AM in the morning according to the position of the Sun. I packed up and climbed down to the valley of Bee Loud Ground. After three hours, I reached the center of the valley. I could see nothing but heavy bushes, dotted with some flowering plants and orchids. The sky was clear. There was a ridge with a tree line high above. I decided to sit on the grass and have some berries for breakfast. It was a lovely scene around. Suddenly, I could hear humming sounds. It sounded like a swarm of bees. At first, I could not see anything. I got a glimpse of seven small drones flying high from the slopes to the center of the valley. I swiftly entered the bushes and lay low. I could hear them shooting past over me. Those probably had high-resolution cameras on them and belonged to the Chinese side. This was the secret of the Bee Loud Ground.

Once the drones were gone, I waited for an hour and did a long monkey crawl up the valley, and the skin of my palms and hands was shredded by the sharp stones and thorny undergrowth. After about half an hour on the move, I stopped. I was sure that I had been spotted, and soon the drones would come flying after me. I remained hidden for about an hour behind a fallen pine tree on a slope. Soon, clouds were moving in to my advantage. I got up and started climbing up. After three hours of climbing, I was still not out of the valley. It was getting dark, and I dared not pitch a camp in case the Red Army sent scouts searching for me. I found a small crevice on a steep rocky face surrounded by pine trees. I decided to crawl in. It was moist, and I had no repellent. Fortunately, the drones were the only "insects" I encountered that day in the valley. It began to snow. I was not given anything which would bring questions to the enemy's mind if I was caught. That night, I covered myself up with whatever wool and plastic for the tent I had brought with me. The wind was whistling, and I was a shriveled-up firefly in the land of the snow flies, which can survive at -9 degrees Celsius. It was terribly freezing. I had a runny nose and a burning forehead. I was worried; I still had half the mission to be done.

Morning found me with an aching body and a heavy head. I packed up and headed out of the valley. Before midday, I was out of it. I started towards my next point, the listening station. After an hour of trekking, I found a spot that was supposed to be near my destination. The weather was clear, and I could scan the heavily wooded mountains. There seemed to be a concrete structure jutting out of the vegetation just about 2 km far on the opposite mountain. I was not confident, as I was feeling terrible with my fever. I thought of progressing and viewing it from a closer point. The last thing I remembered then was my legs not being able to hold me any longer, and I felt like a log about to fall.

On waking up, I found myself lying on a wooden bed in a room with stone walls, and a ceiling with hymns written on it. My breathing was heavy; I felt the cough in my lungs. Was I now among the Chinese? I could not move my head; it felt like a stone. Some sort of covering was there on the right side of my head. Was it bandage? Probably the guys from the listening station had found me after I fell. I moved my legs in an attempt to get down. There was excruciating pain in my right ankle. I fell unconscious again. I woke up to the sound of Buddhist hymns being chanted. The Chinese army praying for forgiveness for trespassing against us?

A monk came, he had a bright face as if light was radiating from it, and asked me in Dzongkha how my head felt. I told him I was alright. He told me that a woodcutter, coming to the monastery, had found me unconscious with a bleeding head and brought me on his donkey to the monastery. I had been unconscious for 3 days. Three days! What would happen to my mission? I tried to get up, but the monk pushed me firmly but slowly down. He said that I was lucky to be alive. I had a high fever running when the woodcutter brought me in. I had serious congestion in my chest. I was in a semi-coma stage. It was the chief monk, who was an expert in herbal medicine, who had restored me. I said I had no idea that for 3 days I was unconscious. It seemed to me like just half a day. He told me to stop talking and lie quietly as I was not well and the chief monk had provided strict advisory regarding my rest and medicines. I passed out before the monk could complete his sentence.

I woke up to find no one in the room. Handmade candles were lit, along with a few oil lamps. My breathing was still heavy. My head and ankle were in pain. I tried hard and got up. There was a dry, cold wind coming from behind a screen. I went behind it and found a closed door and a closed window. The window was broken; I tried to see through the gap. Outside, it was pitch black. I went back to the bed. I was limping and having difficulty breathing. Which monastery was this? Where were my belongings, scriptures, and the coded prayer flags? What was my location? How far was I from my last location near the mountain, I was partially sure I had a glimpse of the secret Chinese listening station, When would I be fit enough to get out? My mission was the first priority. The door opened, and the monk who had come in earlier was surprised to see me sitting up. He had a cane basket and a stone glass. He said it was time for my oral medicine to begin, and he also had two types of ointments: one to be applied to my chest and another for my head. While he removed the covering on my head, it was very painful. It was not a bandage but a long leaf of some tree with herbal medicine on it. He changed it and put a new one. There was a lasting burning sensation. I was given three pellets, which I gulped down with water. The water seemed a bit warm. He told me to lie down and sleep. He said the pellets I had would put me to sleep.

It was probably 3 a.m. when I awoke. I felt that the burning sensation on my head was gone; the head felt heavy no more. The chest congestion and ankle were still not fully recovered. It was foolish even to think that it would go away so soon. I lay staring at the hymns written above. The candles were at their last legs, and there was not enough light. I fell asleep. The sound of the door opening awakened me. Someone was trying to open the window. Sunlight poured in. A monk came up. He was old, with wrinkled skin on his face but had eagle eyes with a strange brightness in them. Even his face glowed like the monk who had dressed my wounds the previous night. He did not speak, but he touched my head, then put his hand on my chest, and then ran his fingers over my right foot. He gestured for me to get up. He gave me some pieces of cucumber with some sort of bitter oil on them. I obeyed. He broke his silence and said he knew why I was here. I shrunk. Did he know my identity? The next moment, he said that I had come to find out myself and free myself from the confusions I had been harboring for a long time. He said that I should not be around this place for long, and he would make arrangements for me to return to my familiar place as soon as possible. He said this was not a place for me to stay. This region belonged to people who had shed their self and were there for serving others, by showing them the right path to salvation. I said that I was also a monk and had the same convictions. His eyes seemed to look through me into infinity. I was immobile. Was it hypnotism? However, it went away. He told me to come out with him to the prayer hall. I followed him, limping. I sat along with the other monks. All had the same radiance on their faces.

After the prayer was over, the chief monk told me to come with him to his chamber. On entering, I saw the room with a stack of herbs on one side and a wooden rack made by an amateur carpenter, on which there were bundles of scriptures. There was minimal furniture. A low table with crooked legs, small glass bottles with colorful liquids, and a few handmade candles in one corner. The room had a large window. I looked out and saw that the monastery was located on a hump in a deep valley with snow-peaked mountains on all sides. I could not spot a single footpath or house in the vicinity. Had I reached Shambala? I was not that pure. I read in the old scriptures that only those who were free from any kind of sins and desires would be able to find it and achieve immortality, a blissful state. Did the Shambalians give me an entry by mistake? Well, I was a man who, of course, had desires and had committed sins—though not serious ones—before joining the regular army from AWES. After that, I was a member of a special operations unit carrying out secret executions across the border. There was blood on my hands.

The monk sat on the floor near the window and ushered me to sit in front of him. I sat. He looked at me with his bright deep sight. He said, "Are you thinking that you are in the land of purity where there is eternal bliss?" I was stunned. I had thought about Shambala or Gyanganj just a moment ago. Was he a counterintelligence officer from the Chinese side? I replied in the negative. I continued normally, saying that I was just a monk from a small monastery near Gelephu. I expected that he would ask me the details of the monastery there to verify. I was ready with the answers. I had been trained well, and details were provided to me so that, in the face of an interview, I would be able to keep my camouflage impenetrable. The monk did not dig further. He said, "You are where your mind is." He said that a man must realize himself before realizing the world and God. If he fails in understanding himself, if he fails to subdue the contradictions within himself, then he will not be able to see his future path and destination clearly. He will falter now and then and be fighting against his own shadow forever. The monk was speaking, and I was listening motionless, as if in a trance. He added that the world around us is ours; no land, no man is foreign. We all are, in fact, together. We put up silly walls of borders and of continents. The whole creation is ours to exist. We just live and die with childish ideas of difference, jealousy, greed, and lust. Therefore, I, as a monk, should only strive for excellence, refinement of my spirit, and achieve knowledge of universal light, and show the path to people who are caught up in the quagmire, bent upon harming each other.

A sudden gust of cold wind ran in through the window, and I shook, as if I awoke from a dream. The monk looked back at the window and said that it would snow that day. He said that as I was limping and still having difficulty breathing, I required rest, but not here. He would make arrangements for me to go back to my monastery in Gelephu. He added that if I would like to refine myself and begin my upward journey to the state of Nirvana and have no traces of Samsara left in me, then he would make arrangements for me there in his monastery. I would have more and more light coming into my mundane soul. I said that it would not be possible. I had many duties to perform. I had a special camp on meditation coming up in my monastery at Gelephu very soon. I had to return within the next two days. The monk said, "You cannot be in all places all at once like Lord Krishna does. Krishna had once stunned Brahma by showing him that he had made innumerable Brahmas and was the master of innumerable universes all at once. Lord Krishna has access to all the cosmic verses that float in the Karna ocean." I was surprised. This man in front of me was thorough with Hindu mythology. The monk smiled and asked if I would want to be like Lord Krishna. I replied that I was too busy with my work at the monastery at Gelephu and was having a hard time coping. I would not want such large areas as universes under me. I am just a firefly, flying here and there. The monk said that even an apparently insignificant firefly flying about in the darkness of the forest challenges the darkness with its little light. It is little, but it spreads brightness where darkness seems to rule supreme. That was a noble job too. I said that here in this monastery, it seems I have moved back to the ancient past with not a single movement of the modern world near me. Whereas in Gelephu, we have the seclusion at our monastery, but we get a window to the modern world too. Wasn't it better to keep a slight contact with the progressing world? I always have a chance of spreading the enlightenment that I receive through meditation and worship of Lord Buddha.

The monk smiled and said that one should know that the modern times do not always bring things for the first time before us. There are fundamental truths which we think the modern scientist discovered for the first time, like John Dalton's atomic theory of 1808, which in fact was discovered 2500 years ago by Rishi Kashyap. Therefore, we should not be too sure of what our senses tell us; they may not be showing us the truth all the time. He further stated that he agreed with my idea of spreading the individual enlightenment received to the people outside our track, though it may attract only a few genuine listeners. He rang a small brass bell, and a monk came in. He gave him instructions to take me back to my room and give me the necessary medicines on time so that I would be fit for the down journey soon. He even instructed him to ensure that I did not go out of my room. Perhaps he did not want me to see the entire monastery. Perhaps there were secrets hidden.

I was back in my room. I looked through the window, clouds were approaching like stormy sea waves. The monk closed the door, window, and went away. I was given some boiled potatoes with butter for lunch. I fell asleep. The monk came in the evening and gave me medicines. I saw that my small bag with the polythene sheet, prayer flags, and dry food which I had carried, was there in one corner. Were all of them members of the Red Army, disguised as monks, as I was a disguised soldier? Was this monastery working as the listening station? Had they discovered the codes on the prayer flags, which came in a combination of colors and thread work, blended in with the prayers? Had they decoded it? With these possibilities, I would have slim chances of getting out of here. The monk who was attending to me came in after dusk, lit new oil lamps, and gave me cucumber with some sort of oil on it, and mashed potatoes with smelly butter. He gave me an extra yak wool blanket. He told me that I must preserve the heat of the food and medicines I received that day within me, as it would help me in my journey downwards through the extreme cold weather. That night, I slept soundly.

All the oil lamps had extinguished themselves. I think it was almost past midday when I awoke. I looked through the crack in the window, and it was still foggy outside and extremely cold. I tried to calculate the days I had exhausted. Perhaps it was the 6th or 9th or 18th day of my mission. I had lost track of time and days. The door was shut from outside. I looked up at my prayer flags; all the codes were there. I emptied my dry food container. I thought that if they were not real monks, there would be a chance that they would put a microchip transmitter in them. They would track me on my journey down. There was no such thing. I put all the edibles back in.

That day, I was not allowed outside; it kept snowing through the day. At lunch, I was given mashed potatoes and cucumber. The chief monk came in and ate with me. While eating, he asked whether I was feeling alright. I said I was fine, except for a slight pain in my ankle, in my head, and a bit of cough in my lungs. After lunch, he gave me some medicines. He said that it was very cold outside and these would keep me warm. He told me to lie down and left.

The next thing I saw was two men carrying me across the snow. They put me in a tent. I felt that my body had gone numb. I tried to raise my hand but I could not. I lost consciousness. When I awoke again, I saw four men examining me closely. One of them grinned to see me awake and rushed out, calling someone. Another man came in and told me that I was saved. They were Zhops. They had found me after the snowstorm stopped. They had gone to find some lost cattle and found me leaning against a pine tree. They caught sight of me in the white snow because of the colorful prayer flags in which I was wrapped. The snow had buried me chest-deep. I asked which day it was. They looked confused. They lifted my hands and showed the frostbites. It had made my fingers blackish, and they told me that my feet also had frostbites. I would have to be carried down on a makeshift stretcher they had made with branches and cloth. They had no medicines with them, so they would take me to the nearest village. I asked for my bag, which contained my prayer flags of codes and food. They showed it to me. I told them to empty it and show me the contents. Everything was there, they also put in the bag the large prayer flags in which I was wrapped. They said that the area in which they found me is out of their routine tracks, they usually do not venture there, as the Big Foot has been often seen or heard there.

I slept through the day. When I awoke, I was terribly hungry as if I had not eaten for days. Some sort of soup was pushed with a wooden ladle into my mouth. It was not enough; I told them I needed solid food, but they disagreed and said something about my condition. I was too weak to make out fully.

The next day, I woke up and found my body swinging in the stretcher being carried down. At one point, the Zhops stopped; they gave me some butter to eat. I demanded more, and they gave me dried yak milk solids. Then we moved on again. At dusk, we reached the village. I was attended by some medicine man. He drew his inference by putting his ear on my chest, his fingers on my temples, and examined my hands and feet. At night, I sat up to drink hot soup and a full bowl of mashed potatoes and gulped down the prescribed pellets. The next day, the Zhops told me that my frostbites were too serious. The medicine man had said that I should be taken to a town where I could get the attention of modern medicine. I told them that I belonged to the monastery at Gelephu and would like to be taken down there. I was again on the stretcher, journeying through the deep green valleys. There were nine Zhops who were given the duty of reaching me to Gelephu.

After about two and a half days' journey, I was suffering from severe backache accompanied by pain in my feet and fingers. Finally, I was inside the monastery at Gelephu. The contacts inside the monastery instantly informed their associates outside, and within 9 hours, a team of three Bhutanese men came in and took me in a car with a Bhutanese number plate. I lay on the back seat. On my way down, I was given an injection, probably a sedative. Later, I learned that I was passed through the checkpoints as a sick Bhutanese monk being taken to India for emergency treatment. Once on the Indian side, near Bongaigaon, I was shifted to a different vehicle with an Indian civilian number plate and taken to Hasimara airbase. After 6 hours of drive from Bongaigaon, I was admitted to the airbase hospital, and it was there that I regained full consciousness.

The doctors there treated me for frostbites and chest congestion. A small chunk of flesh from my right foot was surgically removed. My fingers were treated. I looked like a leper with bandages on my feet and fingers. I asked the nurse there for my bag. She said that she did not know about it. An intelligence officer came in on the ninth day of my hospital stay and talked to me. He told me that I was expected to return after 18 days, but I was found at Gelephu after 36 days had passed. I was wonderstruck. I guessed that it was the 12th day of my mission when I had a talk with the chief monk at that unknown monastery. I had lost track of time and days at that time. One or two days might have been missed, but not so many days. I asked for my bag, and he said that it was in the right hands and I was not to worry about it. The officer told me that I would be taken to another location soon. I requested him about making a call to my parents. He denied it and said that I would not be allowed to contact or talk with anyone until my debriefing was over.

After I regained my ability to walk and all the congestion was gone, I had my bandages removed. Soon, I was put on a military C-130. It took me to a heavily fortified airbase. The small cottage allotted to me had a cook and an attendant. I was pretty comfortable there but longed to get in touch with my parents, the guys of my unit, and, of course, Dipannita. One evening, the top brass who sent us off from the soft station near Bomdilla came in. We had a long exchange. I told them about the swarm drones at the Bee Loud Ground, about the hill where I suspected a concrete structure was hiding behind trees, and the monastery where the monks revived me. They listened, made notes, and audio recordings. A map of the area was spread out, and I tried my best to point out the location where I was on the morning when I tripped and fell unconscious. They listened with rapt attention to the exchanges I had with the chief monk of the monastery where I was nursed. They opened up digital files, live satellite feeds projecting the terrain map of northeast Bhutan. They shook their heads and whispered to each other. They said there was no monastery anywhere near the location to which I was pointing. I remembered the old monk saying that it is not necessary that all the time our senses show us what is true and real. At the end of the debriefing, they agreed about the swarm drones, but I could not convince them that all I said about the monastery was not a hallucination under the snow where I must have remained for days. I told them about the large prayer flags in which I was wrapped. They said they had examined them, and they were just ordinary prayer flags. Before leaving, they told me that I was not to make any calls to anyone until further orders would reach me about communication with my near and dear ones.

The next day, I was awaited on the runway by a military Mi-8. When I boarded the chopper, a crew member handed me a brown envelope. I read the contents. It was an order of joining as an officer in the Army Intelligence Branch. I would be posted at Babunia Cantonment. While at Babunia, after the formalities were over, I was given an officer's cottage with attendants and a car. While I was at the office on the sixth day of my new job, I received a phone call that I was free to call my parents and friends but remain absolutely silent about my previous assignment. I did call my parents the next moment, and they said that they had been communicated earlier by the army informing them that I was safe and sound. They asked me about my long silence, and I said that it was due to routine work. I remembered Dipannita's number, and I rang her. Her response was not as stern as it used to be. She said that she had thought she would never be able to see me again. She was eager to know how I was and where I was. I said that I would meet her soon. Dipannita said that she had received orders to join a base hospital in Udaipur within the next seven days. I told her that I would meet her at Udaipur as soon as I would get some days off. She said that she would be very happy to meet the firefly which was still glowing in the dark.